Original title:
Holding on to Hope

Copyright © 2024 Swan Charm
All rights reserved.

Author: Liina Liblikas
ISBN HARDBACK: 978-9916-89-901-4
ISBN PAPERBACK: 978-9916-89-902-1
ISBN EBOOK: 978-9916-89-903-8

A Cherished Promise

In shadows deep, Your light does shine,
A whispered vow, forever mine.
Through trials faced, my heart will cling,
To sacred truths, Your love does bring.

With every breath, a song of grace,
In silent prayer, I seek Your face.
The dawn will break, the dark will flee,
A cherished promise, You hold me free.

When Flowers Bend Yet Stand

In fields of green, when storms do rise,
The flowers bend beneath dark skies.
Yet in their bow, a strength is found,
They reach for light, from hallowed ground.

With every tear, a petal falls,
But still, they dance to Heaven's calls.
Their fragrant hope, a testament,
To grace that blooms, a life well spent.

Echoes of the Divine

In stillness found, the whispers flow,
With every beat, the heart will know.
The echoes call, a soothing balm,
In sacred spaces, spirits calm.

Through trials faced, we rise anew,
In love's embrace, the pure and true.
With open souls, we learn to see,
The echoes of the divine in me.

Spirit's Weathered Compass

With weathered hands, the compass shows,
The path of faith that steadfast goes.
Through storms and winds, it guides the way,
To shores of peace, come what may.

In every choice, a lesson learned,
The spirit searches, forever yearned.
With every step, we seek the light,
A compass true, in darkest night.

Wings of Assurance

In shadows deep, we find our light,
A promise whispered, day and night.
With faith as our guide, we rise and soar,
On wings of assurance, forevermore.

Through trials faced, our hearts entwined,
In prayer and hope, true peace we find.
Each moment cherished, grace intertwined,
In love's embrace, our souls aligned.

Echoes of a Brighter Tomorrow

In the silence, a soft voice calls,
To rise above, where no heart falls.
The echoes of hope, a melody sweet,
Guiding our steps, where dreams and paths meet.

With every dawn, new mercies flow,
A canvas painted, with colors aglow.
Emboldened we stand, through trials faced,
In unity found, our fears replaced.

Beneath Heaven's Veil

Under heaven's veil, we find our grace,
Each soul a story, a sacred place.
In moments still, the spirit sings,
A tapestry woven, through all life's strings.

With love as our anchor, we journey on,
In laughter and tears, we are all one.
The light may flicker, yet never die,
For beneath heaven's veil, we learn to fly.

Radiance in Despair

In darkest night, a beacon gleams,
A reminder of hope, a thousand dreams.
For even in shadows, love will prevail,
A radiance bright, when hearts exhale.

With every struggle, we find our worth,
In moments fractured, we rebirth.
Through trials faced, our spirits raised,
In radiance found, forever praised.

Covenant of the Faithful

In heart's embrace, we gather here,
With voices raised, we cast out fear.
A promise shared, through trials faced,
In faith we stand, our lives interlaced.

United by grace, we walk the way,
In shadows deep, we find the day.
With every step, in joy we tread,
The covenant blooms, where Love is fed.

A Lantern in the Night

Upon the path, a light does shine,
A beacon bright, our hearts entwined.
In darkest hours, hope's flame persists,
Guiding us forth with gentle twists.

Each flicker tells of love's embrace,
A steady hand in sacred space.
Together we rise, with spirits bold,
A lantern's glow, our truth unfolds.

The Tapestry of Trust

Woven with care, each thread we share,
A tapestry rich, stitched with prayer.
In colors bright, our stories blend,
A gift of Love, that has no end.

Through trials faced, and joys we've known,
In woven hearts, our faith has grown.
Together we weave, in harmony's song,
A tapestry rich, where we belong.

Threads of Light

In every heart, a thread of gold,
A shining hope, a tale retold.
With gentle hands, we weave anew,
Threads of light, in love, we pursue.

Through valleys low and mountains high,
We walk together, our spirits fly.
Each thread a bond, in fervent trust,
In sacred light, we find what's just.

Embrace of the Divine

In shadows deep, Your light will shine,
With gentle hands, You create the divine.
Each whispered prayer, a sacred song,
In Your embrace, I forever belong.

Through valleys low, and mountains high,
Your love enfolds, like the vast sky.
I seek Your grace, in every dawn,
In every breath, Your love goes on.

Threads of Promise

In every heart, a thread so fine,
Woven with care, by hands divine.
Through trials faced, and joys we find,
A tapestry of hope, forever entwined.

With every stitch, a story told,
Of faith and dreams, in hues of gold.
In silent moments, Your promise glows,
In each heartbeat, Your love bestows.

In the Arms of Serenity

In stillness found, a sacred place,
Wrapped in peace, I seek Your grace.
With every sigh, my worries cease,
In Your embrace, I find my peace.

Beyond the chaos, a gentle stream,
Flowing softly, like a dream.
In tender whispers, You call my name,
In the arms of serenity, I'll never blame.

The Everlasting Flame

A flicker small, yet fiercely bright,
Your love ignites the darkest night.
In every heart, a flame does dwell,
A burning truth, these tales we tell.

Through storms that rage, and winds that howl,
Your fire stays, it will not scowl.
With every breath, the warmth remains,
The everlasting flame, love sustains.

The Echo of Tomorrow

In the quiet dawn, hope does rise,
Promises whisper through the skies.
Each breath a prayer, a sacred chance,
Guiding our souls in a blessed dance.

Faith weaves softly, a tapestry bright,
Shadows of doubt fade with the light.
In unity's song we shall abide,
With love as our compass, hearts open wide.

Moments entwine, a divine embrace,
Time echoes truth in this sacred space.
With each step forward, we choose to believe,
In echoes of tomorrow, we shall receive.

Born from Ashes

From the ashes of sorrow, we rise anew,
Forged in the fires of trials we knew.
With wings of resilience, we take to the skies,
Embracing the dawn, where our spirit lies.

The burdens we carried, now light as a song,
In the heart's embrace, we learn to belong.
With every heartbeat, a rhythm of grace,
Reborn in hope, we find our place.

The scars of the past, a testament's truth,
In the garden of life, blossoms our youth.
Together we journey, hand in hand so free,
Born from the ashes, we cherish the sea.

Serenity's Pathway

Walk gently upon this serene pathway,
Where whispers of peace guide us each day.
In the stillness of night, faith's lantern glows,
Illuminating the love that forever flows.

With each step taken, let burdens release,
In the soft embrace of the heart's sweet peace.
Nature's song echoes through silent trees,
A hymn of devotion carried by the breeze.

Here wisdom whispers, in shadows of grace,
As we find our way through time and space.
With open hearts, we dare to explore,
On serenity's pathway, we learn to restore.

A Tender Flame's Glow

In the darkness of night, a flame softly gleams,
A tender reminder of hope's waking dreams.
With each flicker of light, love's warmth we feel,
Guiding our spirits, a promise to heal.

The fire within us ignites with each breath,
Shining through shadows, defying all death.
In communion with stillness, our hearts intertwine,
As embers of kindness in silence align.

In the circle of grace, we gather as one,
A tapestry woven, our souls brightly spun.
With compassion as fuel, we kindle the night,
A tender flame's glow reveals the divine light.

The Garden of Renewal

In the quiet dawn, life awakens,
Petals kissed by dew, glisten bright.
Each seed planted, hope roots deep,
In the arms of grace, we find our light.

Whispers of love through the branches,
The sun caresses the earth with care.
Every flower a prayer, every breeze a hymn,
In this sacred space, we lay bare.

Gentle rains wash the weary soul,
Every droplet a promise, pure and bold.
Life's cycles teach us, in nature's embrace,
The garden reveals the truth of old.

Yet shadows dance in the golden light,
The trials faced, our hearts refine.
From ashes and dust, we rise once more,
In the garden's solace, our spirits align.

With open arms, the Creator waits,
In the whispers of leaves, we hear the call.
Trust in the process, renew the heart,
In the garden of renewal, we find it all.

Sanctuary Among the Storms

When thunder rumbles, and shadows fall,
To the heart's refuge, we seek to flee.
A quiet haven amidst the chaos,
In faith we gather, united and free.

Each drop of rain, a cleansing tear,
A reminder that storms, too, shall pass.
We hold each other through darkest nights,
In love's embrace, our fears we amass.

The lighthouse stands on the rugged shore,
A beacon of hope in turbulent seas.
Though waves may crash, and winds may howl,
In the sanctity of faith, we find our ease.

With every struggle, our spirits grow,
Resilience blooms in the trials we face.
In the eye of the storm, we find our peace,
A sanctuary carved by divine grace.

Together we rise, through tempests strong,
Trusting the path that leads us on.
In every storm, we learn to believe,
A sanctuary among the storms is never gone.

Pillars of Belief

On the foundation of faith, we stand tall,
Pillars of belief, strong and true.
In unity, we rise, with hearts entwined,
Guiding our spirits to all we pursue.

Each prayer a stone, each promise a beam,
Constructing a temple, steadfast and bright.
In the shadow of doubt, we build our trust,
A fortress of love, dispelling the night.

Through trials and tears, our resolve will grow,
In each challenge faced, we find our way.
With hope as our mortar, we build the walls,
In the light of grace, we shall not sway.

Together we sing, our voices as one,
In harmony, we create our song.
With each note sung, our spirits take flight,
In the pillars of belief, we all belong.

As the dawn breaks, the shadows recede,
We stand in the light, together we thrive.
For in every heart, the spirit ignites,
Pillars of belief shall ever survive.

The Promise of Morning

As night fades softly, dreams take flight,
Whispers of dawn paint the sky so wide.
With every sunrise, a promise renewed,
In the stillness, hope and love abide.

Golden rays pierce the misty veil,
Casting away the worries of night.
The warmth of day brings warmth to the soul,
In the promise of morning, all feels right.

Each breath a gift, each moment a chance,
To cherish the journey, the love we sow.
In the light that spreads with each new chance,
The promise of morning helps us grow.

With hearts aligned, we greet the sun,
A tapestry woven of light and grace.
In every dawn, we find our purpose,
The promise of morning, our sacred space.

So let us rise with the breaking day,
To witness the beauty that life affords.
In every moment, let gratitude flow,
For the promise of morning, our spirit restores.

Nightingale's Call

In the stillness, whispers rise,
A nightingale beneath the skies.
Songs of hope, a gentle sway,
Calling souls to find their way.

Through the shadows, light will gleam,
Guiding hearts to sacred dreams.
Each note a prayer, softly told,
A melody of faith, so bold.

In the darkness, hear the sound,
Awakening the lost, the found.
With wings of grace, the spirit flies,
In every heart, the Nightingale cries.

Trust the echoes, find your strength,
In harmony's embrace, great length.
For every tear, a song will rise,
Illuminating starry skies.

Let the nightingale inspire,
Igniting in us holy fire.
Travel on, with hope anew,
In every song, the truth shines through.

The Refuge of Faith

In troubled times, we seek the light,
A refuge found in prayer's delight.
Wings of faith, so fiercely spread,
Through darkest paths, the spirit's led.

With each step, hear the calling,
In quiet whispers, fears are falling.
Trust the promise, hold it dear,
In the sanctuary, love draws near.

Walls of doubt may close us in,
Yet in the shadows, peace begins.
Embrace the stillness, find your way,
In faith's embrace, we will not stray.

Gathered hearts in unity,
Strengthened by community.
Through storms we walk, hand in hand,
In the sanctuary, we stand.

With open arms, the refuge waits,
Forgiveness flows, as grace translates.
In every prayer, hope is reignited,
In the arms of faith, we are united.

Heartbeats of the Divine

In silence, listen, softly beat,
The pulse of love in every street.
With every breath, a sacred flow,
The heart of God, we come to know.

The rhythm echoes, pure and strong,
In each beat, we find our song.
Bound by the grace that intertwines,
Our spirits dance, in sacred signs.

Through trials faced, we learn to trust,
In every challenge, love is just.
The heart's desire, a guiding star,
Leading us home, no matter how far.

With open hearts, we draw the line,
In heartbeats heard, the voice divine.
We gather strength, as we believe,
In every moment, love we weave.

As dawn awakens, hearts will rise,
To greet the day with joyful cries.
For in each heartbeat lies the sign,
Of boundless love, the divine design.

The Embrace of a Dream

In the twilight, visions bloom,
Whispers soft dispel the gloom.
Dreams like stars, they light the way,
To realms where love can freely play.

With every sigh, the heart takes flight,
Embracing visions bathed in light.
In sacred dreams, the spirit soars,
Discovering love forevermore.

Trust the magic, let it guide,
In the embrace, you'll find your stride.
For dreams are portals to the soul,
Where every whisper makes us whole.

In union with the cosmic thread,
Every heartbeat gently led.
Together, we shall weave our fate,
In love's embrace, we celebrate.

Awakened dreams, a tender grace,
In every heartbeat, find your place.
For life's a journey, rich and grand,
With open hearts, let dreams expand.

Beneath the Stars of Faith

In the quiet night we pray,
Guided by the stars' bright sway.
Each twinkle whispers hope so grand,
Embracing souls in His gentle hand.

Beneath the heavens vast and wide,
Hearts unite, no need to hide.
The light within, a burning flame,
In faith, we rise, we call His name.

Branches sway with timeless grace,
In every heart, He finds His place.
With every breath, we seek the way,
In darkness, still, we find the day.

Promises like stars above,
Shine down upon us, purest love.
In the stillness, faith will grow,
Through trials faced, His truth we know.

Eager spirits, lift your gaze,
Feel His presence, endless praise.
In unison, our voices blend,
Beneath the stars, our hearts ascend.

The Whispering Winds of Change

Beneath the boughs, the winds do blow,
Carrying whispers of change to sow.
Each breeze a sign, divine and true,
Inviting souls to start anew.

In gentle shades, the spirit speaks,
Encouraging the humble, the meek.
With every rustle, hope abounds,
In nature's song, His love resounds.

Mountains rise, yet valleys low,
In every heart, His mercy flows.
Through shifting winds, we walk in light,
Our path made clear, our fears take flight.

Let us embrace what must unfold,
For in His hands, our stories told.
With open hearts, we bravely stand,
The winds of change, guided by His hand.

So let the breezes carry dreams,
Through every soul, His love redeems.
In joyful dance, let spirits soar,
For change is but a heavenly door.

A Journey through the Shadows

In shadows deep, we seek the light,
A journey wrought with silent fight.
Each step we take may feel alone,
Yet in the dark, His love is shown.

Through valleys low and mountains high,
With trembling hearts, we reach the sky.
His guiding hand, a lantern bright,
Illuminates our path with might.

In struggles faced, our faith grows strong,
In every trial, we belong.
For shadows deepen, yet they fade,
As dawn breaks through, His truth broadcast.

As night gives way to morning's hue,
With every day, He makes us new.
In every shadow, grace prevails,
Amidst the storms, His love never fails.

So take this journey, brave and true,
For with each step, we come to view,
A tapestry of grace unfurled,
In shadows, we embrace the world.

Celestial Embrace

In the heavens, a love divine,
Stars align, their paths combine.
With every heartbeat, close we feel,
A celestial embrace, His love is real.

The moon whispers secrets at night,
In every beam, there shines a light.
Through cosmic dance, hearts intertwine,
In the vastness, we are His design.

With every prayer, we float above,
Connected by threads of endless love.
In the silence, our spirits unite,
In celestial embrace, pure delight.

Lift up your voice, let praises soar,
In harmony, forevermore.
For in His arms, we find our place,
In every breath, a sacred space.

So gaze upon the starry dome,
Feel in your heart you are not alone.
In this embrace, forever stay,
In celestial love, we find our way.

The Faintest Glimmer

In shadows deep, a spark does gleam,
A light that whispers hope's sweet dream.
In darkest nights, the heart can see,
A faintest glimmer, guiding me.

Through trials fierce, my soul takes flight,
In faith's embrace, I find my light.
Each tear and sigh, a prayer to share,
A longing heart finds solace there.

When tempests rage and fears arise,
My spirit lifts to sacred skies.
With every breath, a song I sing,
To greet the dawn that love will bring.

In quietude, I seek the way,
Where mercy flows, and shadows sway.
The glimmer grows, my path is clear,
In every pulse, the Lord is near.

Eternal grace, my hands do raise,
In grateful heart, I rest and praise.
For every moment, joy anew,
The faintest glimmer shines right through.

Threads of Eternity

In woven tales of time and space,
Dances a thread of boundless grace.
Each life a verse in love's great rhyme,
Stitched in the fabric of pure time.

Weaving together, hand in hand,
In every heart, a sacred strand.
Through light and dark, we journey on,
With faith as guide, till shadows gone.

A tapestry of dreams unfolds,
With stories rich, and courage bold.
In every twist, a purpose clear,
The threads of hope draw us near.

In prayer we find the strength to rise,
Letting love weave through our skies.
In knitted hearts, we learn to share,
Threads of eternity everywhere.

As seasons turn and moments flow,
In every stitch, our spirits grow.
With grace as thread, no fray, no tear,
In love's embrace, we are laid bare.

Faith's Gentle Embrace

In quiet nights, my spirit bows,
To faith's soft whisper, humbly vows.
With open heart, I seek the truth,
A gentle love that knows no ruth.

Through trials faced and storms endured,
In faith's embrace, my soul is cured.
With every step, a promise made,
In light and grace, my fears do fade.

In sunlit days, or shadows cast,
I trust the path that's meant to last.
With tender hands, the heavens guide,
In faith's sweet embrace, I will abide.

Each tear a jewel of prayer's delight,
In darkness turned, my heart takes flight.
With joy I walk, with spirit free,
In faith's embrace, my soul shall be.

In love's warm glow, I find my peace,
A gentle faith that will not cease.
For every moment speaks of grace,
In faith's embrace, I find my place.

Whispers of Promise

In the stillness, whispers soar,
Echoes of promise, forevermore.
In every heart, a sacred vow,
To seek the love in this moment now.

As dawn breaks soft, the world awakes,
In whispered breaths, my spirit shakes.
With every bloom, a truth unveiled,
In hope anew, love has prevailed.

Through valleys low and mountains high,
The whispers call, and I comply.
A journey shared, hand in hand,
In every step, faith takes a stand.

With every star that lights the night,
A promise shines, guiding light.
In every soul, a story told,
Whispers of promise, brave and bold.

Together we rise, together we pray,
In love's embrace, we find our way.
In every heartbeat, truths align,
Whispers of promise, forever shine.

Through Unfamiliar Valleys

In valleys deep, where shadows dwell,
I wander forth, my heart a shell.
Yet whispers rise in twilight's glow,
A guiding light, where grace does flow.

The mountains loom, their heights I fear,
But faith within will draw me near.
Each step I take through vale unseen,
Is cradled in love's gentle sheen.

With every stone, a lesson learned,
Through trials faced, my spirit burned.
The path ahead, though dark it seems,
Is lit by hope and lofty dreams.

In secret groves, His presence found,
Where echoes of His grace abound.
I tread anew, with fervent breath,
Through valleys life, and there find rest.

So onward still, my soul shall soar,
Through unfamiliar, sacred lore.
For in each valley, He awaits,
To guide my heart, to open gates.

The Abiding Whisper

In silent nights, a whisper calls,
Through shadowed paths, my spirit falls.
A beckoning soft, a promise near,
In quietude, I hold Him dear.

With every gust of twilight breeze,
His voice does sway the trembling trees.
In moments spent beneath the stars,
I find my peace, my sacred scars.

Each dawn that breaks, the world anew,
His gentle touch, my strength in view.
With every heartbeat, every sigh,
I sense His love that will not die.

Though tempests rage and doubts arise,
In abiding trust, my spirit flies.
For in the stillness, He resides,
A faithful guide where hope abides.

Through trials faced, His wisdom shared,
In every ache, I feel prepared.
The whisper lingers, deep and true,
A bond of grace that sees me through.

The Heart's Gentle Resolve

With every dawn, my spirit wakes,
In quiet strength, my resolve breaks.
To love the world, both near and far,
To see His light, my guiding star.

Amidst the dark, where shadows creep,
My heart will stand, my faith will leap.
In kindness shared and mercy shown,
The seeds of love are softly sown.

Each step I take, a vow renews,
With gentle hands, I weave the hues.
In every song the angels sing,
I feel the pulse of nature's wing.

Through trials faced, my heart holds tight,
In every tear, a spark of light.
For love, it blooms in fierce embrace,
A gentle shield, a holy grace.

Though storms may rise and tempests lash,
In faith, I stand, my fears will pass.
The heart's resolve, a living flame,
In every breath, I speak His name.

Threads of Grace

In whispered prayers, the heart does weave,
A tapestry of love, one can believe.
Through trials faced, the spirit holds,
A thread of grace, His promise unfolds.

Each tear that drops, a blessing grows,
In shadows cast, His presence shows.
Through storms that rage, He calms the seas,
In quiet whispers, we find our ease.

With every step, the journey sings,
A sacred dance, where hope takes wings.
In valleys low, His hand extends,
We rise renewed, as darkness bends.

The light within, it guides our way,
Through darkest nights, to dawn of day.
In love's embrace, we find our home,
In threads of grace, we are not alone.

The Ascent of Belief

Upon the mountain, faith does rise,
With eager hearts and hopeful eyes.
Each step we take, a promise bright,
The ascent of belief, a sacred flight.

Through trials faced, we lift our gaze,
In every struggle, we seek His praise.
With prayerful hearts, we climb each stone,
In unity, we find our own.

A summit calls, and fears recede,
In trust, we find what souls do need.
With every breath, the Spirit leads,
In the ascent, our hearts are freed.

The view unfolds, a kingdom near,
In laughter sweet, in silent cheer.
For in belief, we learn to soar,
In the ascent of love, forevermore.

A Well of Enduring Light

Deep in our souls, a well resides,
Of enduring light, that never hides.
In moments bleak, it shines anew,
A beacon bright, forever true.

When shadows fall, and doubts arise,
It casts away the darkest skies.
With every drop, our spirits swell,
In the well of light, all hearts can dwell.

Through trials faced, we sip our fill,
A taste of hope, serene and still.
In every dawn, it shines so clear,
A promise kept, we draw it near.

So let it flow, this light divine,
In every heart, a sacred sign.
A well of grace, forever bright,
In busyness, find your peace each night.

The Serene Path

A path unfolds in quiet grace,
Where every turn reveals His face.
With gentle steps, we walk in trust,
Upon this road, our spirits gust.

Through fields of gold and skies of blue,
The serene path, a gift anew.
In every flower, His touch we find,
A trail of love, where hearts unwind.

In whispered winds, His voice speaks low,
Guiding our steps, where grace shall flow.
With every breath, we seek the light,
On the serene path, all hearts take flight.

So journey on, through day and night,
With faith as anchor, hearts alight.
For on this way, we'll learn to see,
The beauty found in unity.

Light in the Abyss

In darkness deep, His light shall shine,
Guiding hearts to paths divine.
Though shadows loom and fears arise,
Hope ignites, a flame in skies.

With every prayer, a whispered plea,
A soul restored, a spirit free.
In trials faced, we find our grace,
Light in the abyss, His warm embrace.

Through valleys low, through mountains high,
Let faith be the compass, never shy.
For in the night, His promise glows,
A beacon bright, where love bestows.

So walk with courage, hearts alight,
With every step, embrace the fight.
In silent moments, let Him speak,
The light in the abyss, strong yet meek.

Eternal flame that will not fade,
A sanctuary, firmly laid.
In shadows cast, let hope persist,
For in His arms, we shall exist.

The Seed of Tomorrow

In every heart, a seed is sown,
A whisper from the great unknown.
Nurtured by faith, watered with love,
A promise blooms from realms above.

Through trials faced and storms endured,
In every struggle, our souls matured.
The harvest waits, a bountiful grace,
In patience found, we'll find our place.

With every dawn, new hope does rise,
Awakening dreams beneath the skies.
As we tend the garden of our days,
Let kindness guide us in all ways.

For every seed has time to grow,
In soil of faith, let blessings flow.
Trust in the plan, as we sow deep,
The seed of tomorrow, our souls to keep.

So lift your eyes to the coming light,
In every shadow, find the bright.
For in the earth, we plant with care,
A legacy of love to share.

Wings of Belief

Upon the winds of faith we soar,
With wings of belief, to heights we explore.
Casting aside all doubt and fear,
In the embrace of hope, we draw near.

With every prayer, we rise above,
Seeking the path of peace and love.
In trials faced, our spirits take flight,
Guided by whispers of sacred light.

The burdens we carry become our strength,
In the journey's curve, we go to great lengths.
With hearts united, we spread our wings,
In the harmony of hope, love sings.

So trust the journey, the steps we trace,
With wings of belief, we find our place.
In unity's bond, our spirits entwine,
Together we soar, in grace divine.

With every dawn, new beginnings arise,
Through skies of trials, our spirits fly high.
In the dance of faith, we find our way,
Wings of belief shall never sway.

When Shadows Fall Away

When shadows fall and darkness sighs,
In whispered prayers, our spirits rise.
For in the night, His light appears,
A gentle balm to heal our fears.

With faith as anchor, we stand tall,
In love's embrace, we shall not fall.
With every tear, a hope unfolds,
In stories written, the truth is told.

Through valleys deep and mountains steep,
In silent trust, the promises keep.
For even in the deepest night,
His grace surrounds, a guiding light.

And when the dawn begins to break,
In every heart, new hopes awake.
As shadows fade, the day shall glow,
With every step, His love we'll know.

So let us walk with hearts aglow,
In the warmth of faith, let courage flow.
For when shadows fall and fade away,
In His embrace, we find our way.

Wings of Transparency

In the light of truth, we soar,
With open hearts, forevermore.
Beneath the gaze of heaven's eye,
Our spirits lift, as eagles fly.

Through trials deep, we come to find,
The clarity of love, divine.
Each feather glistens, pure and bright,
Our souls take flight in holy light.

In whispers soft, the truth reveals,
The sacred bond that grace conceals.
With wings unfurled, we rise anew,
Embracing faith in all we do.

As shadows fade, the dawn breaks clear,
Our hearts aligned, we persevere.
In every breath, the Spirit's call,
We find our strength, we rise, we fall.

With wings of light, our journeys weave,
In every moment, we believe.
Together bound by holy ties,
We dance in joy, where love never dies.

The Hand That Guides

In every moment, near or far,
A gentle touch, our guiding star.
In trials faced, we see the hand,
That leads us to a promised land.

Through stormy seas and winds that blow,
The hand that guides will ever show.
With every step, a whisper clear,
In faith we walk, devoid of fear.

When shadows cast their darkened veil,
We trust the hand that will not fail.
In love's embrace, we find our way,
Through night and dark into the day.

A beacon bright, through life we tread,
The hand that guides, where others dread.
In every heart, a flame ignites,
With hope renewed, our spirit fights.

Together, we shall rise and sing,
In every trial, His love we bring.
The hand that guides will lead us home,
In unity, we shall not roam.

Trusting Through the Clouds

As clouds arise, we look above,
To find the light of peace and love.
In faith we stand, though storms may roar,
Trusting still, for we are sure.

With every tear, a lesson learned,
Through heartache deep, our spirit yearned.
We seek the silver lining bright,
A promise kept through darkest night.

In whispers soft, the Spirit speaks,
In quiet moments, strength it seeks.
Through veils of doubt, we find the way,
With trusting hearts, we shall not sway.

From every cloud, a grace bestowed,
In patient love, our hearts bestowed.
With open arms, we greet the dawn,
In every heart, our hope is drawn.

Through trials faced, we rise as one,
With faith intact, 'til day is done.
Trusting through clouds, we find our peace,
In love's embrace, our fears shall cease.

Soul's Quietude

In silence sweet, the spirit glows,
A sacred space where stillness flows.
In whispered prayers, the heart takes flight,
Finding solace in the night.

The world may shout, but here we find,
A quiet realm, both calm and kind.
With open hearts, we sit and breathe,
In soul's quietude, we find reprieve.

In gentle grace, the moments pause,
Reflecting on love's truest cause.
In every sigh, the peace descends,
Binding our hearts, as time transcends.

Through every breath, the Spirit sighs,
In tranquil waves, our spirit lies.
As stars above begin to gleam,
We find the truth within our dream.

With quiet souls, we shall unite,
In harmony, our hearts take flight.
In stillness deep, our love will reign,
In joy we dwell, free from all pain.

Voices of the Faithful

In quiet corners, we gather as one,
Whispers of grace, the battle is won.
Hearts intertwined, we sing His praise,
In the glow of hope, our spirits raise.

Each tear we shed, a prayer in the night,
Carried on wings, to the heavens' light.
Though shadows may fall, His love will stay,
Guiding us home, through night into day.

In storms of doubt, we find our song,
Together in faith, we ever belong.
Voices united, we stand so tall,
For in His presence, we can never fall.

Through valleys of sorrow, His joy will break,
With every heartbeat, His love we make.
The power of prayer, a fortress so strong,
In the choir of the faithful, we find our song.

The Path Through Trials

Upon the road where shadows creep,
We tread with faith, our promises keep.
Each step a lesson, each fall a rise,
In struggle we find, our spirit flies.

Through fire and storm, we will not yield,
In the Lord's grace, our wounds are healed.
The path is narrow, yet leads us home,
In every heartache, we are not alone.

Courage our banner, love as our guide,
Walking in truth, we will not hide.
In valleys bleak, His light shines bright,
As we journey forth, embraced by His might.

Each strife a blessing, each trial a gift,
Transforming our hearts, giving our spirits a lift.
With eyes on the heavens, we march on high,
For in His arms, we learn to fly.

Crowned with Light

In the silence of dawn, His glory shines,
Awakening souls, drawing hearts in lines.
Crowned with light, we rise and proclaim,
In the embrace of love, we call His name.

The stars above, like diamonds so bright,
Reflect His promise, illuminating the night.
With every breath, we join the refrain,
In the rhythm of life, His love we gain.

Hearts aglow with the fire divine,
Walking in faith, our spirits entwine.
Crowned with light, we stand unafraid,
For in this journey, new paths are laid.

Through trials we rise, empowered and free,
Sons and daughters of grace, destined to be.
With crowns of light upon our brow,
In His presence, we flourish now.

The Sky that Waits

Under the expanse where the eagles soar,
We gaze at the sky, our spirits explore.
In the hush of the night, we find His grace,
The heavens open, welcoming our face.

Each star a promise, each cloud a prayer,
Whispers of hope in the cool night air.
The sky that waits, a canvas so wide,
Holding our dreams, where love will abide.

Through storms of life, His hand holds fast,
Reminding us gently, our trials won't last.
With every sunrise comes light anew,
Painting our hearts in shades of His view.

We walk with courage, our heads held high,
For beneath His wings, we're never shy.
The sky that waits is a promise so bright,
Guiding our journey, transforming the night.

The Bridge of Grace

Crossing over the silent stream,
Where whispers of mercy softly gleam.
Each step is taken with faith anew,
On a bridge of grace, we seek the true.

The sun breaks forth from the darkest night,
Illuminating paths with holy light.
Here souls come weary, yet find their rest,
On the bridge of grace, they are truly blessed.

Trusting the flow of the endless tide,
With hearts open wide, we walk side by side.
In the love that binds, we find our strength,
As we journey together, we go the length.

Every heart healed, every tear replaced,
In the arms of love, we are embraced.
Together we rise, in joy's warm place,
Bound forever on the bridge of grace.

With each new dawn, let praises soar,
For the gift of grace, forevermore.
In unity's song, our spirits find,
A bridge that leads us to the divine.

A Heart That Remembers

In the whispering winds, where memories flow,
A heart that remembers, tender and slow.
Each moment cherished, like stars in the night,
Guiding our journey with warm, gentle light.

Through valleys of longing, through shadows we tread,
A heart that remembers, where angels have led.
In the laughter of children, in love's tender call,
We find the reflections of life's glorious thrall.

Time gracefully weaves the threads of our past,
A tapestry rich, its colors steadfast.
In joy and in sorrow, in peace and in strife,
A heart that remembers embraces our life.

Every lesson learned, every tear we shed,
The heartbeat of wisdom, where hope is fed.
In silence, we gather the gifts of our days,
In a heart that remembers, love's song always plays.

Holding the echoes of days gone before,
A heart that remembers is never unsure.
As we journey onward, both humble and grand,
In love's boundless memory, together we stand.

In the Quiet of Promise

In the quiet of promise, where dreams gently rest,
Hope whispers softly, inviting the blessed.
Each moment suspended, a sacred embrace,
In the stillness of faith, we find our place.

With shadows retreating, as daylight breaks free,
In the quiet of promise, we learn how to be.
In the hush of a prayer, our hearts intertwine,
Finding strength in the silence, a love divine.

Here in the stillness, the world fades away,
In the quiet of promise, we learn how to pray.
Each thought a reflection, each breath a new vow,
In the peace of the moment, we live in the now.

The whispers of hope guide our fragile hearts,
In the quiet of promise, where true grace imparts.
Though storms may still come, and shadows may loom,
In the heart of the promise, we'll rise from the gloom.

So let us be silent, let us listen well,
In the quiet of promise, within us shall swell.
A symphony of faith that sings through the night,
A promise of dawn and the coming of light.

Miracles Amid the Storm

In the heart of the tempest, where thunder roars loud,
Miracles unfold, wrapped in shadows shroud.
Every drop of rain brings a blessing anew,
As grace flows freely, like morning's soft dew.

When hope seems elusive, and fears take their toll,
Miracles arise, igniting the soul.
In the chaos of voices that clash and contend,
A quiet assurance declares, "I will mend."

With eyes turned to heavens, we seek the divine,
In moments of hardship, the stars brightly shine.
Through trials and struggles, our spirits will soar,
As miracles dance on the storm's distant shore.

In the depth of despair, where faith may grow thin,
Miracles whisper, "You shall rise again."
Every wave that crashes, every fear we face,
Holds a glimmer of truth, a sweet gift of grace.

So when storms are raging, we lean on His word,
For miracles happen when hearts are stirred.
With every heartbeat, may we find the way,
To see miracles bloom, come what may.

A Tapestry of Trust

In the quiet folds of faith, we weave,
Threads of hope that we believe.
Each moment stitched in love's embrace,
United hearts find their place.

Through trials faced and storms we bear,
A tapestry, rich and rare.
God's hand guides with gentle grace,
In every thread, his calm we trace.

Trust blooms in the darkest night,
A guiding star, our shared light.
In sacred bonds, we stand as one,
Until the journey's work is done.

Through laughter shared and sorrows deep,
In our hearts, his promises keep.
Together we rise, as angels sing,
In the tapestry, joy takes wing.

So let us gather, hand in hand,
In this sacred, fertile land.
With trust, we weave our lives anew,
A shared vision of love, so true.

Streams in the Desert

In arid lands where hope seems lost,
God plants a seed, though cold the frost.
From barren soil, life springs anew,
A stream of grace flows gently through.

With every step upon this earth,
We carry forth a sacred birth.
In desolation, we find the light,
Watering the dreams that took flight.

In the silence, hear His voice,
In the troubling times, rejoice.
For even in the driest hour,
His love descends like rain, a shower.

Paths of hope in the sand we trace,
Leading us to His warm embrace.
Rivers run where once was pain,
In the desert, peace regains.

Trust the journey, lean on grace,
For in the wilderness, we find our place.
With faith, we drink from life's pure stream,
In God's hands, we dare to dream.

The Beacon of Souls

In the twilight glow of setting sun,
A beacon shines for everyone.
Guiding lost hearts to the shore,
Illuminating paths to explore.

Its light, a whisper in the night,
Bringing shadows into sight.
Calling faithful to unite,
In love's embrace, hearts take flight.

Each soul a spark, a song divine,
Connected in a love sublime.
Together, we kindle the flame,
Transforming the world in His name.

From distant shores to near and far,
We carry forth His guiding star.
In service, we shine our light bright,
A beacon of hope, a radiant sight.

So let us gather, strong and bold,
In every heart, His truth unfold.
Together, we rise, souls entwine,
In the glow of love, forever shine.

Lighthouses of the Spirit

Upon the cliffs where storms do swell,
Stand lighthouses, our hearts compel.
Guiding ships through turbulent tides,
With steady beams, love abides.

Through surging waves and winds that roar,
We hold our faith, we seek for more.
Each light a prayer, a sacred call,
In darkest nights, we will not fall.

The spirit's lamp shall never dim,
In every struggle, we find Him.
A refuge built on love's pure might,
Together, we triumph in sacred light.

With every call across the sea,
We shine for those who yearn to be.
In every soul, a lighthouse stands,
As love extends to all the lands.

Let faith illuminate our way,
In every heart, His warmth will stay.
Together we are, forever bright,
Lighthouses of the spirit, pure light.

The Soul's Portrait of Trust

In silent prayer, I seek your grace,
With every breath, I find my place.
A tapestry of hope unwinds,
In trusting love, my heart defines.

The whispered winds, they carry truth,
Through trials faced, I cling to youth.
Each step I take, your light I trace,
In faith I stand, in your embrace.

When shadows loom, and doubts arise,
I lift my gaze to endless skies.
For in the dark, your voice ignites,
With courage born from loving sights.

The storms may rage, they will not sway,
The bond we share will guide my way.
In every battle, I will find,
My soul's portrait, gently aligned.

Through years of grace, through tears I've shed,
Each thread of trust, just like you said.
With open hands, my heart I give,
In your embrace, my spirit lives.

When the Path is Dark

In moments hushed, when shadows creep,
I seek your light, a promise deep.
With every step, a prayer I weave,
In faith, I trust, I will believe.

The road ahead may twist and turn,
Yet in my heart, your fire burns.
With every tear, a lesson grows,
Your love, a river that ever flows.

Through valleys low and mountains high,
I lift my voice, I raise it nigh.
In darkest hours, your hand I hold,
A story of faith, forever told.

The night may stretch, the silence reigns,
Yet in my soul, your light remains.
With every doubt, I find the way,
In trust I walk, come what may.

So lead me on, with gentle care,
Through every moment, I know you're there.
In love profound, I find my spark,
Your guiding flame amidst the dark.

The Rise of the Muted Flame

In stillness forged, a flicker glows,
A hidden strength that only knows.
Though winds may howl and shadows loom,
The silent flame will break the gloom.

From ashes cold, it dares to rise,
Each whisper caught in tender sighs.
With gentle warmth, it lights the way,
A beacon bright in disarray.

Through trials faced and voices hushed,
In quiet moments, spirits rushed.
Each spark ignites a longing deep,
Awakening dreams that yearn to leap.

In unity, we gather near,
With hearts ablaze, we cast out fear.
No longer muted, the flame will soar,
Together we stand, forevermore.

So cherish light, embrace the spark,
In every heart, dispel the dark.
For love ignites the flame anew,
In silent strength, we rise for you.

A Heart Open to the Divine

In sacred space, my heart unfolds,
With open arms, your love enfolds.
Each whispered prayer, a gentle plea,
To dance within your mystery.

The beauty found in every breath,
Awakens life, transcends all death.
In moments still, I hear the call,
As grace descends, I feel it all.

With every beat, my spirit grows,
In joy and sorrow, life bestows.
An open heart, your light to claim,
Illuminates this sacred flame.

In kindness shared, in love expressed,
I find my truth, I feel blessed.
With gratitude, I rise and sing,
A soul in tune with everything.

So let me walk this path with grace,
In every moment, seek your face.
With open heart and open mind,
I find my peace, in you I'm blind.

Echoes of a Prayer

In silence, we gather, hearts entwined,
Whispers of faith, in the night they bind.
With each breath, we reach to the sky,
Echoes of prayers, as stars drift by.

Beneath the moon's glow, our spirits rise,
Seeking the truth hidden in lies.
Hands held high, in unity strong,
Together we sing, the sacred song.

Through trials faced, we find our way,
In shadows cast, we seek the day.
With hope as our guide, we chart the seas,
In every heartbeat, our souls find ease.

In moments fleeting, love takes hold,
In cherished stories, our faith unfolds.
The whispers of angels, gentle and near,
In echoes of prayer, our spirits steer.

With every dawn, a chance to renew,
In the strength we share, our purpose is true.
Together we stand, a radiant light,
In the grace of our bonds, we find our might.

The Rise of Dawn

As darkness retreats, the sky begins to glow,
A promise awakens, in the light we sow.
Birds take to flight, in joyous embrace,
The rise of dawn, a holy grace.

With each sunbeam, old fears dissipate,
Through trials of night, we rejuvenate.
In sacred silence, the world anew,
Guided by faith, we know what is true.

Mountains stand tall, yet we shall not fall,
In the heart of despair, we hear His call.
Like flowers in bloom, with colors so bright,
We rise in the morn, embracing the light.

The heavens above, a canvas divine,
In every sunrise, our souls intertwine.
With gratitude sung, our spirits arise,
In the dance of time, we witness the prize.

Each moment we breathe, a chance to reflect,
In the warmth of the sun, our souls reconnect.
The rise of dawn, a beacon so clear,
In its radiant glow, we conquer our fear.

Embracing the Unseen

In the depths of silence, where love abides,
Lies the sacred wisdom that our soul confides.
Though eyes may not see, the heart knows the truth,
Embracing the unseen, we find our youth.

The whispers of angels blend with the breeze,
In moments of stillness, we find inner peace.
With faith as our guide, we venture beyond,
In the beauty of grace, our spirits respond.

Through trials and storms, we learn to believe,
In shadows of doubt, we find ways to cleave.
Knowing that strength is often concealed,
Embracing the unseen, the heart is revealed.

In the tapestry woven with threads of the soul,
We gather the fragments, and make ourselves whole.
The unseen is present, in love, it is found,
In the dance of the spirit, our joy knows no bound.

Each heartbeat a promise, each breath a prayer,
In the stillness of life, we discover our care.
Embracing the unseen, we cherish the light,
In the sacred connection, our souls take flight.

Sacred Roots of Resilience

Deep in the earth, where our stories begin,
The sacred roots grow, through loss and through sin.
In the struggle and strife, we find our way,
The strength of resilience guides us each day.

When storms rage around, and shadows draw near,
We stand firm and strong, casting away fear.
Through the whispers of ages, wisdom unfolds,
In the roots of our spirit, our courage upholds.

With love as our anchor, we weather the gale,
In unity found, we shall never fail.
The bonds that we forge, through trials define,
In sacred resilience, our hearts intertwine.

As trees reach for heaven, we too strive to grow,
With faith in our hearts, we nourish the glow.
Through seasons of change, our spirit shall thrive,
With sacred roots deep, we feel so alive.

In the beauty of struggle, our stories unite,
With the wisdom of ages, we rise to the light.
Sacred roots of resilience, a blessing bestowed,
In the journey of life, let our truth be our road.

Anchored in the Unknown

In the depths where shadows play,
Faith finds courage, night and day.
Hidden paths that lead us near,
To the whispers we hold dear.

Every step, a sacred dance,
Guided by a silent chance.
Hearts entwined in faith's strong thread,
Finding light where spirits tread.

Through the storms that seek to blind,
Truth unfolds for those who bind.
In the vastness, hope ignites,
Shattering the darkest nights.

Immersed in grace, we stand tall,
Listening closely to the call.
Beyond the veil of what we see,
Faith becomes our destiny.

With each breath, the journey breathes,
Love is sown in spirit's leaves.
Anchored firm, though all seems lost,
We embrace the holy cost.

Spirits Woven in Light

In a tapestry of bright stars,
We find strength in our memoirs.
Souls united, a sacred band,
Guided by a higher hand.

Through the corridors of grace,
We see love in every face.
Every heart a glowing spark,
Illuminating paths so dark.

Woven threads of joy and pain,
In this dance, we lose and gain.
Radiance in every tear,
For love's echo draws us near.

In a world that yearns for peace,
May our spirits find release.
Bound by faith, we rise and soar,
In sacred bonds forevermore.

With hope's light as our refrain,
We'll embrace the joy and pain.
Spirits woven, hand in hand,
In the fabric of this land.

Beneath the Heavens' Watch

Beneath the heavens vast and wide,
We seek solace, peace, and guide.
Every star a silent prayer,
Echoing our longing air.

In the night, our spirits rise,
Cloaked in dreams that touch the skies.
Faithful hearts, we stand as one,
Beneath the moon, our battles won.

Whispers of divinity flow,
In the gentle breeze that blows.
Nature sings of love's embrace,
In every flower's tender grace.

As we ponder life's great quest,
In stillness, we find sacred rest.
Beneath the heavens' watchful sight,
Our souls are cradled in the light.

Together, we ignite the night,
In unity, we find our might.
Under stars, we make our plea,
Forever bound, forever free.

A Song in the Silence

In the stillness, whispers play,
A song emerges from the gray.
Hearts attuned to heaven's grace,
Finding peace in quiet space.

In the silence, love unfolds,
Gentle stories to be told.
Every note, a sacred thread,
Binding souls in words unsaid.

In moments when the world stands still,
We hear echoes of love's will.
A melody that softly calls,
In hushed tones, the spirit falls.

With each heartbeat, tune us right,
Guided by that inner light.
A song emerges from the deep,
Cradling all that we keep.

In the silence, hope resides,
A current in the rising tides.
May we cherish every song,
Finding strength to carry on.

A Covenant of Comfort

In shadows deep, Your light does shine,
A shield, a guide, forever mine.
With whispers soft, You call my name,
In faith I walk, through joy and pain.

Your promises like stars above,
In every trial, I feel Your love.
A haven built on trust and grace,
In Your embrace, I find my place.

With every tear, You count them all,
In gentle grace, You lift my fall.
A covenant, a sacred thread,
In hearts united, we are led.

Through valleys low, I do not fear,
Your presence strong, forever near.
With faith as wings, I soar above,
In every moment, bound by love.

So here I stand, my heart laid bare,
In every prayer, I find You there.
A covenant so pure and true,
In every breath, I worship You.

The Dance of Destiny

Beneath the stars, our fates entwined,
In rhythm's grace, Your ways defined.
With every step, Your hand in mine,
We dance in hope, through space and time.

The music swells, a sacred song,
In heartbeats chanting, we belong.
With every turn, we find our place,
In love's embrace, we seek Your face.

In trials faced, we sway and spin,
With strength from You, we rise again.
For in this dance of joy and pain,
Your guiding light will always reign.

As shadows shift, our spirits soar,
With every leap, we crave You more.
In destiny's weave, we see the plan,
A sacred dance, hand in hand.

So let us twirl in faith's delight,
Through darkest hours, toward the light.
In every moment, let love lead,
Together bound, in You we're freed.

Illuminated Hearts

In quiet prayer, our spirits rise,
With radiant hope, we touch the skies.
Your love ignites the darkened night,
In every heart, a guiding light.

Together we seek, in faith fulfilled,
With every whisper, our souls are thrilled.
In sacred truths, we find our way,
Illuminated by love each day.

Through trials faced, Your warmth we crave,
In steadfast grace, You help us brave.
With open hearts, we journey far,
Reflecting love, our morning star.

In moments still, we hear Your call,
With softened hearts, we give our all.
Illuminated in shared embrace,
In unity, we find our space.

So let us shine, a beacon bright,
In every soul, Your love ignite.
Together we rise, with fervent start,
In every breath, Your grace, our art.

The Chosen Way

The chosen path, where shadows flee,
In faith we walk, as one with Thee.
With every step, our hearts aligned,
In love and truth, our souls defined.

Through trials fierce, we lift our gaze,
In darkest nights, You are our praise.
A journey made, with purpose clear,
With faith as guide, we have no fear.

In sacred moments, we find our voice,
In every challenge, we rejoice.
For You, O Lord, are always near,
In whispered grace, we hold You dear.

The chosen way, a path of light,
With open hearts, we chase the fight.
In unity, our spirits soar,
Together bound, forevermore.

So lead us on, we pledge our all,
In love's embrace, we will not fall.
The chosen way, forever sung,
In every heart, a hymn is strung.

Faith's Gentle Whisper

In the stillness of the night,
A whisper tells of hope so bright.
Hearts entwined in quiet prayer,
Love surrounds, a sacred air.

Through every doubt that clouds the way,
A gentle voice begins to sway.
Trust in the path that leads you home,
In His embrace, you're never alone.

When storm clouds gather, fear takes flight,
Look within for guiding light.
In the chaos, peace unfolds,
Faith's warmth, a truth that holds.

Each tear we shed, a drop of grace,
In trials faced, we find our place.
Together lifted, spirits soar,
In love's vast ocean, we explore.

So lean on faith, let doubts dissolve,
For in His love, our hearts evolve.
A gentle whisper, soft and clear,
In every moment, He is near.

The Light Beyond Shadows

In the darkness where fears reside,
Hope ignites, a holy guide.
A flicker bright, where shadows play,
The dawn breaks forth, a brand new day.

Within our hearts, a flame will rise,
Through trials faced, we see the skies.
With every step, the path is shown,
In love's embrace, we are not alone.

Beneath the stars, in quiet grace,
We seek the light, we find our place.
With faith as strong as mountains high,
We lift our eyes and dare to fly.

Every whisper, every prayer,
Carries hope upon the air.
No shadow deep can dim the glow,
For in His love, our spirits grow.

So venture forth, let courage reign,
In darkest nights, there's no more pain.
The light that shines will guide our way,
To brighter shores, come what may.

Cradled by Grace

In the arms of love we find,
A gentle touch, so warm, so kind.
Through every trial, every tear,
He cradles us, dispelling fear.

With every heartbeat, we are blessed,
In grace's arms, we find our rest.
The journey long, yet never bleak,
For faith's sweet whispers gently speak.

In moments lost, His light restores,
A beacon bright that ever soars.
With faith as our loving guide,
In His embrace, we shall abide.

Through valleys low and mountains tall,
His presence reigns, it conquers all.
Cradled by grace, we rise anew,
In every dawn, blessings accrue.

So take His hand, don't walk alone,
In love's embrace, we find our home.
Together woven, souls entwined,
In grace's heart, true peace we find.

When Dawn Breaks the Night

When silence falls, and stars collide,
Hope awakens, dreams abide.
The night may whisper tales of fright,
Yet dawn descends, bringing light.

In every shadow, faith will gleam,
Guiding hearts, igniting dream.
With every pulse, a prayer ascends,
In love's embrace, our spirits mend.

The golden rays break through the dark,
A gentle touch ignites the spark.
In every sigh, in every flight,
Hope is born when dawn breaks the night.

Through trials faced and endless fears,
Each tear transformed, a world appears.
In love's sweet promise, we find light,
A sacred bond that shines so bright.

Let not the night hold you in chains,
For dawn will rise, and hope remains.
With every heartbeat, we ignite,
A brighter world when dawn breaks the night.

In the Embrace of Being

In quiet grace, I find my soul,
A gentle whisper, making me whole.
The light around, a sacred hue,
Reminds me of all I'm called to do.

Nature speaks in every tree,
In rustling leaves, I hear the plea.
To cherish life in every breath,
In love and peace, I find life's depth.

With open heart, I seek the way,
Guided by stars that light the day.
The universe, a vibrant song,
In its embrace, I feel I belong.

As silence falls, my spirit soars,
I touch the realm of ancient shores.
A banquet set for those who see,
The sacred dance of you and me.

In every dawn, new hope is found,
In the embrace where love is crowned.
Together we rise, hand in hand,
In the embrace of being, we stand.

Faith Reflections

In shadows deep, faith lights the way,
A guiding star in night's array.
Each trial faced, a sacred trust,
In every moment, rise from dust.

The heart remembers, the spirit seeks,
In whispered prayers, my soul speaks.
Through storm and calm, I walk the path,
In faith's embrace, escape the wrath.

With eyes set high, I see the grace,
The endless love that I embrace.
A tapestry of dreams unfurled,
In faith, I touch the boundless world.

The quiet moments, still and bright,
Reveal the truth behind the light.
In every tear, a lesson learned,
In every heart, a flame that burned.

In faith reflections, strength appears,
A constant flow, like rivers clear.
Together we rise, hearts aligned,
In the sacred bond, love intertwined.

The Weaver's Hands

In gentle fingers, threads combine,
A tapestry of life divine.
Each color tells a story bold,
In the weaver's hands, futures unfold.

With every stitch, a prayer is sewn,
In vibrant hues, we are not alone.
The fabric strong, a sacred blend,
In love's embrace, the threads extend.

The loom of life, both strong and frail,
In joy and sorrow, we set sail.
With every twist, a lesson learned,
In the weaver's hands, our hearts discerned.

From strands of doubt, to hope's bright shine,
In unity, our lives entwine.
Each moment shared, a sacred art,
In the weaver's hands, we play our part.

As patterns shift, and seasons change,
We find the beauty in the strange.
With every heartbeat, we shall stand,
In the warmth of the weaver's hands.

Slumbering Dreams

In twilight's glow, the spirit rests,
In slumbering dreams, the heart invests.
A sacred journey through the night,
Unveiling truths in starry light.

With whispered hopes, we drift away,
To realms where night becomes the day.
Each vision speaks of love and grace,
In slumbering dreams, we find our place.

The moonlight's touch, a gentle weave,
In quiet moments, we believe.
Through shadows deep, a dance unfolds,
With every breath, the dream retold.

In visions bright, the spirit flies,
With every star that fills the skies.
We seek our truth, the soul's delight,
In slumbering dreams, the heart takes flight.

Awake, refreshed, the dawn appears,
In every dream, we conquer fears.
With faith renewed, we stand as one,
In slumbering dreams, our journey's begun.

Stars That Light the Path

In the night, they softly shine,
Guiding hearts through dark divine.
Each twinkle tells a sacred tale,
Of love's embrace in every gale.

With whispers sweet, they call us near,
Their luminescence, clear and dear.
A lantern set in heaven's seam,
Leading souls to hope's bright dream.

The vast expanse, a canvas wide,
Each star a promise, faith our guide.
In every struggle, they ignite,
The courage needed to take flight.

As time unfolds, their glow remains,
A testament through joys and pains.
Beneath their watch, we find our way,
In darkness, they forever stay.

Together we shall rise and soar,
With spirited hearts that seek to explore.
For every step beneath their gaze,
We bask in love's eternal praise.

Beneath Worn Wings

Under the weight of weary flight,
Lies a strength born of purest light.
With every feather, stories weave,
Of sacrifice, this heart believes.

Beneath the skies, in shadows cast,
Worn wings show tales of journeys past.
Yet in the struggle, grace does dwell,
A gentle touch of heaven's bell.

When storms arise, and fears take form,
These wings will shield, and keep us warm.
Embraced by faith, we rise anew,
With every battle, a clearer view.

So soar we must, with spirits bold,
Embracing warmth in every cold.
For underneath those wings of grace,
We find our joy, our quiet place.

United in hope, we learn and grow,
For love is the seed we continually sow.
With every flap, we learn to trust,
In dusty paths, our spirits thrust.

The Unseen Strength

In silence, there lies a gentle might,
A force unseen, yet ever bright.
It lifts us high on weary days,
In unseen arms, we find our ways.

Through trials faced, the heart shall know,
Invisible roots help us to grow.
In whispered prayers, we find our peace,
And from our burdens, we seek release.

Though shadows loom and doubts may rise,
The spirit whispers, true, and wise.
With every heartbeat, strength we gain,
In faith we walk through joy and pain.

A river flows where strength abides,
And in that stream, our hope resides.
Though unseen, it guides our souls,
Crafting life's sacred, weaving roles.

Embrace that power, let it soar,
With every step, we seek for more.
The unseen strength will lead the way,
In love's embrace, we shall not sway.

Eternal Whispers

In quiet moments, echoes play,
Whispers of love that never stray.
Through endless time, they softly hum,
A melody of all that's come.

Each breath a prayer, each sigh a song,
In heartbeats, we've belonged so long.
Eternal whispers guide our quest,
To seek and find, to love, to rest.

In the gentle breeze, they flow so sweet,
Carrying hope on dancing feet.
With every touch of twilight's grace,
We find the light, a warm embrace.

As dawn unfolds the day ahead,
Those whispers linger, softly spread.
In every corner of our souls,
They forge the path, they make us whole.

So listen close, for they are near,
Eternal truths we need to hear.
In love's soft voice, let us abide,
With whispers worn, our faithful guide.

Graceful Resilience

In trials we rise, with faith we embrace,
The storms that surround, we find our place.
With each falling tear, in silence we stand,
The light of His love guides our trembling hand.

Through shadows of doubt, we journey along,
The strength in our hearts sings a sacred song.
In whispers of grace, we gather our might,
Fearing not the dark, we return to the light.

Each stumble a lesson, each fall a new start,
In the fabric of life, He stitches the heart.
With courage we face all the trials ahead,
Clothed in His mercy, our spirits are fed.

A tapestry woven with love's gentle thread,
In the depths of despair, the hope is not dead.
Together we rise, hand in hand we ascend,
For grace flows like rivers, beginning that mend.

In every quick breath, in every soft sigh,
We honor the pain, we honor the sky.
Through grace-filled resilience, our spirits ignite,
Forever His children, we bask in His light.

Yearning for the Sacred Dawn

In the quiet of night, our hearts softly plead,
For the dawning light, for the hope that we need.
With whispers of prayer, we lift up our souls,
Yearning for solace that morning unfolds.

The stars up above, like diamonds they gleam,
As we ponder our dreams, we follow the stream.
Each moment of darkness, a promise it seems,
To guide us unerringly back to our dreams.

We seek out the grace in the break of the day,
Where shadows dissolve, and the worries drift away.
With open hearts wide, as the sun starts to rise,
The beauty of worlds fills our questioning eyes.

In the chorus of light, we unite and we sing,
For every new dawn, every joy it can bring.
Together in faith, in His love we are bound,
Our spirits awakened, in harmony found.

So let the sun rise, let it shine ever bright,
As we journey forward, guided by His light.
Each heartbeat a prayer, each step is a song,
In the yearning for dawn, we courageously belong.

The Unseen Hand

In moments of doubt, when the path isn't clear,
We trust in the grace that forever draws near.
An unseen hand guides, though we're blind to the way,
It cradles our spirits, come what may.

Through valleys of sorrow, through peaks of delight,
The presence surrounds us, a balm in the night.
Each twist of our fate, a divine choreography,
An unseen hand weaving our shared tapestry.

When burdens feel heavy, and weight seems too strong,
We lean on His wisdom, where we truly belong.
In whispers of love, we find our reprieve,
A silent assurance that teaches us to believe.

In laughter and tears, in the dance of the day,
We find in the struggle, there's purpose at play.
The unseen hand lifts, it's the heart of the whole,
In the quiet conviction, He nurtures our soul.

So in every moment, through thick and through thin,
Know the unseen hand is the start and the end.
With faith as our anchor, through life's winding race,
We trust in His guidance, we walk in His grace.

Miracles in the Mundane

In simple actions, in the tasks of our day,
Miracles sprout in the soft light of gray.
A smile to a stranger, a hand to a friend,
These moments of kindness, on them we depend.

In breakfast shared slowly, in laughter so bright,
In stories retold, the mundane takes flight.
Within every heartbeat, the sacred ignites,
A glance at the dawn brings the world into sight.

In chores that we dread, in the rhythm of life,
We find hidden wonders that diminish our strife.
When hearts intertwine, miracles bloom,
Transforming the commonplace into fragrant perfume.

In breathing the air, in the smell of fresh rain,
We realize blessings and find joy in the pain.
For miracles often in the ordinary hide,
A gentle reminder that love is our guide.

So cherish these moments, embrace with delight,
In every small gesture, His love shines so bright.
The mundane is sacred, a canvas divine,
In the miracles caught, our spirits will shine.

The Garden of Dreams

In the garden where hope is sown,
Petals whisper of love once known.
Beneath the sky, hearts intertwine,
In sacred soil, our souls align.

Every flower a prayer in bloom,
They dance gently, dispelling gloom.
Graceful tendrils lift us high,
To touch the heavens, we will fly.

The fragrance of faith fills the air,
In this haven, we find our prayer.
With every dawn, new stories rise,
The garden breathes beneath the skies.

Roots entwined, we shall not break,
In love's embrace, no fear we take.
Trusting the light that guides our way,
In the garden, we choose to stay.

And when the night begins to fall,
We gather close, we hear the call.
For in the dark, we still believe,
In dreams that whisper, we shall weave.

Rays Through the Clouds

From shadowed hearts, a light breaks through,
Kissing the earth, igniting truth.
With gentle love, it warms our souls,
The brighter path, it gently tolls.

In moments lost, a glimmer shines,
The promise seen in sacred signs.
Each ray a hope, so pure, so bright,
Guiding us forth from darkest night.

As clouds may gather, fear may rise,
We stand steadfast, we lift our eyes.
For in that warmth, we find our peace,
In rays of grace, our fears release.

Together we walk, hand in hand,
Through valleys deep, across the land.
With faith as our shield, we shall be free,
Rays through the clouds, our destiny.

So let us praise the light we share,
For in our hearts, we find the care.
Through joy and pain, we rise anew,
In every breath, His love shines through.

Sanctified Strength

In trials faced, our spirits grow,
With every test, love's strength we sow.
Amid the storms, we claim our might,
In sacred trust, we shine the light.

Through valleys low and mountains high,
We lift our gaze, we will not sigh.
For in the struggle, souls are forged,
With every step, our faith enlarged.

In unity, we find our way,
Together bound, in prayer we stay.
For in our hearts, we carry fire,
Sanctified strength, our true desire.

No chain can bind, no fear can quell,
The truth we share, our hearts compel.
With hope as our armor, we press on,
In His embrace, we find the dawn.

So raise your voice, let praises ring,
In sacred strength, our spirits sing.
With love as our guide, we shall prevail,
Sanctified strength will never fail.

The Promise in the Waiting

In silence held, we learn to trust,
In every moment, Him we must.
For in the wait, our hearts align,
The promise spoken, divine design.

With every breath, our hopes arise,
A gentle whisper beneath the skies.
In patience, we find the strength to be,
The promise in the waiting sets us free.

Through trials faced, with faith we tread,
Each step a prayer, our spirits fed.
Though shadows loom, we will not fear,
For in the waiting, He draws near.

So lift your eyes to skies above,
Embrace the gifts of His great love.
For all that's lost shall be restored,
The promise in the waiting, our reward.

In time's embrace, we find our way,
Through darkest nights and brightest days.
With hearts attuned, we'll rise and sing,
The promise in the waiting is our king.

Hope's Eternal Thread

In darkness deep, a light does gleam,
A whisper soft, the heart's own dream.
With faith we weave each fragile strand,
Together strong, we make our stand.

Through trials faced, we rise and soar,
With every tear, we seek for more.
The tapestry of love unfolds,
A story sacred, brightly told.

The morning sun breaks through the night,
A promise kept, in faith's pure light.
Each moment shared, a cherished gift,
In hope's embrace, our spirits lift.

When shadows fall, and doubts arise,
We hold the truth that never lies.
A thread of hope, unbroken, true,
In unity, we shall renew.

In every heart, His presence stirs,
A silent prayer, the soul concurs.
Hope's eternal thread binds us tight,
In love's embrace, we find our light.

The Gift of Tomorrow's Breath

In every dawn, a chance appears,
To wash away our deepest fears.
Each breath we take, a sacred sign,
A gift bestowed, His light divine.

The path ahead, though yet untold,
Is wrapped in grace, a promise gold.
With every step, we walk in trust,
In Him we rise, in Him we must.

Let not the weight of sorrow bind,
For hope and joy, we're meant to find.
With open hearts, we greet the day,
In every smile, in every way.

With whispered prayers, our souls ignite,
In darkest times, we seek the light.
The gift of tomorrow waits for all,
In faith's embrace, we rise and call.

So take His hand, and walk anew,
In every breath, let love break through.
For in His arms, we live and thrive,
The gift of life, we shall revive.

In the Shade of Grace

Beneath the branches of His love,
We find our peace, a gift from above.
In shadows cast, our fears recede,
In the shade of grace, our spirits freed.

Each gentle breeze, a soft caress,
In quiet moments, we find rest.
Through trials faced, we stand as one,
In faith, we rise, the battles won.

The world may roar, but here we dwell,
In sacred space, our hearts can swell.
With every tear, a blessing flows,
In the shade of grace, compassion grows.

Together in His sheltering arms,
We find our strength, we find our charms.
In unity, our voices raise,
A hymn of joy, we sing His praise.

So let us walk, hand in hand,
In love and trust, forever stand.
For in His shade, we find our way,
In the light of hope, we choose to stay.

Blossoms of Belief

In gardens where the faithful sow,
The blossoms bloom, their colors glow.
With every seed, a dream takes flight,
In blossoms bright, we see His light.

The fragrance sweet of love divine,
A gentle grace in every line.
Through trials faced, our spirits soar,
In faith we trust, while seas may roar.

Together here, our hearts unite,
In harmony, we seek the right.
With open hands, we share the load,
In every act, our love bestowed.

Amidst the thorns that life may bring,
The flowers dance, and angels sing.
In every heart, His truth reveals,
The sacred path, through love it heals.

So let us gather, side by side,
In blossoms of belief, abide.
With grateful hearts, we raise our song,
In faith and hope, we all belong.

Milton Keynes UK
Ingram Content Group UK Ltd.
UKHW020043271124
451585UK00012B/1018